CLIMBING BUCKET JOURNAL

This Book Belongs To:

_____

_____

_____

My Bucket List

NO.	ACTIVITY	DONE
1		
2		
3		
4		
5		
6		
7		
8		
9		
10		
11		
12		
13		
14		
15		
16		
17		
18		
19		
20		

My Bucket List

NO.	ACTIVITY	DONE
21		
22		
23		
24		
25		
26		
27		
28		
29		
30		
31		
32		
33		
34		
35		
36		
37		
38		
39		
40		

My Bucket List

NO.	ACTIVITY	DONE
41		
42		
43		
44		
45		
46		
47		
48		
49		
50		
51		
52		
53		
54		
55		
56		
57		
58		
59		
60		

My Bucket List

NO.	ACTIVITY	DONE
61		
62		
63		
64		
65		
66		
67		
68		
69		
70		
71		
72		
73		
74		
75		
76		
77		
78		
79		
80		

My Bucket List

NO.	ACTIVITY	DONE
81		
82		
83		
84		
85		
86		
87		
88		
89		
90		
91		
92		
93		
94		
95		
96		
97		
98		
99		
100		

Goal : _____

_____

What I need :

- [ ] _____
- [ ] _____
- [ ] _____
- [ ] _____
- [ ] _____
- [ ] _____
- [ ] _____

Details :

Date : _____

Location : _____

Start Time : _____

End time : _____

With : _____

Difficulty : _____

Weather :

Notes/Thoughts/Memories

_____

_____

_____

_____

_____

_____

_____

_____

_____

I Give This Experience : ☆ ☆ ☆ ☆ ☆

Goal : _____

What I need :

- [ ] _____
- [ ] _____
- [ ] _____
- [ ] _____
- [ ] _____
- [ ] _____
- [ ] _____

Details :

Date : _____

Location : _____

Start Time : _____

End time : _____

With : _____

Difficulty : _____

Weather :

Notes/Thoughts/Memories

_____

_____

_____

_____

_____

_____

_____

_____

_____

I Give This Experience : ☆ ☆ ☆ ☆ ☆

Goal :_____

_____

🎒 What I need :

- ☐ _____
- ☐ _____
- ☐ _____
- ☐ _____
- ☐ _____
- ☐ _____
- ☐ _____

📋 Details :

Date : _____

Location : _____

Start Time : _____

End time : _____

With : _____

Difficulty : _____

Weather : ☀️ ⛅ 🌧️ ❄️

Notes/Thoughts/Memories

_____

_____

_____

_____

_____

_____

_____

_____

I Give This Experience : ☆ ☆ ☆ ☆ ☆

Goal : _____

_____

What I need :

- ☐ _____
- ☐ _____
- ☐ _____
- ☐ _____
- ☐ _____
- ☐ _____
- ☐ _____

Details :

Date : _____
Location : _____
Start Time : _____
End time : _____
With : _____
Difficulty : _____
Weather : ☀ ⛅ 🌧 ❄

Notes/Thoughts/Memories

_____
_____
_____
_____
_____
_____
_____
_____

I Give This Experience : ☆ ☆ ☆ ☆ ☆

Goal : _____

_____

What I need :

- [ ] _____
- [ ] _____
- [ ] _____
- [ ] _____
- [ ] _____
- [ ] _____
- [ ] _____

Details :

Date : _____

Location : _____

Start Time : _____

End time : _____

With : _____

Difficulty : _____

Weather : ☀️ ⛅ 🌧️ ❄️

Notes/Thoughts/Memories

_____

_____

_____

_____

_____

_____

_____

_____

_____

I Give This Experience : ☆ ☆ ☆ ☆ ☆

Goal : _____

_____

What I need :

- [ ] _____
- [ ] _____
- [ ] _____
- [ ] _____
- [ ] _____
- [ ] _____
- [ ] _____

Details :

Date : _____

Location : _____

Start Time : _____

End time : _____

With : _____

Difficulty : _____

Weather : ☀ ⛅ 🌧 🌨

Notes/Thoughts/Memories

_____

_____

_____

_____

_____

_____

_____

_____

I Give This Experience : ☆ ☆ ☆ ☆ ☆

Goal : _____

_____

🎒 What I need :

- ☐ _____
- ☐ _____
- ☐ _____
- ☐ _____
- ☐ _____
- ☐ _____
- ☐ _____

📋 Details :

Date : _____

Location : _____

Start Time : _____

End time : _____

With : _____

Difficulty : _____

Weather : ☀️ ⛅ 🌧️ 🌨️

Notes/Thoughts/Memories

_____

_____

_____

_____

_____

_____

_____

_____

_____

_____

I Give This Experience : ☆ ☆ ☆ ☆ ☆

Goal : _____

What I need :

- ☐ _____
- ☐ _____
- ☐ _____
- ☐ _____
- ☐ _____
- ☐ _____
- ☐ _____

Details :

Date : _____

Location : _____

Start Time : _____

End time : _____

With : _____

Difficulty : _____

Weather : ☀ ⛅ 🌧 ☁❄

Notes/Thoughts/Memories

_____

_____

_____

_____

_____

_____

_____

_____

_____

I Give This Experience : ☆ ☆ ☆ ☆ ☆

Goal : _____

_____

🎒 What I need :

- ☐ _____
- ☐ _____
- ☐ _____
- ☐ _____
- ☐ _____
- ☐ _____
- ☐ _____

📋 Details :

Date : _____

Location : _____

Start Time : _____

End time : _____

With : _____

Difficulty : _____

Weather : ☀️ ⛅ 🌧️ 🌨️

Notes/Thoughts/Memories

_____

_____

_____

_____

_____

_____

_____

_____

_____

I Give This Experience : ☆ ☆ ☆ ☆ ☆

Goal : _____

_____

What I need :

- [ ] _____
- [ ] _____
- [ ] _____
- [ ] _____
- [ ] _____
- [ ] _____
- [ ] _____

Details :

Date : _____

Location : _____

Start Time : _____

End time : _____

With : _____

Difficulty : _____

Weather : ☀ ⛅ 🌧 ❄

Notes/Thoughts/Memories

_____

_____

_____

_____

_____

_____

_____

_____

I Give This Experience : ☆ ☆ ☆ ☆ ☆

Goal : _____
_____

What I need :
- [ ] _____
- [ ] _____
- [ ] _____
- [ ] _____
- [ ] _____
- [ ] _____
- [ ] _____

Details :
Date : _____
Location : _____
Start Time : _____
End time : _____
With : _____
Difficulty : _____
Weather : ☀ ⛅ 🌧 ❄

Notes/Thoughts/Memories
_____
_____
_____
_____
_____
_____
_____
_____
_____

I Give This Experience : ☆ ☆ ☆ ☆ ☆

Goal :_____

What I need :

- [ ] _____
- [ ] _____
- [ ] _____
- [ ] _____
- [ ] _____
- [ ] _____
- [ ] _____

Details :

Date : _____
Location : _____
Start Time : _____
End time : _____
With : _____
Difficulty : _____
Weather :

Notes/Thoughts/Memories

_____
_____
_____
_____
_____
_____
_____
_____

I Give This Experience : ☆ ☆ ☆ ☆ ☆

Goal : _____

_____

What I need :

- [ ] _____
- [ ] _____
- [ ] _____
- [ ] _____
- [ ] _____
- [ ] _____
- [ ] _____

Details :

Date : _____

Location : _____

Start Time : _____

End time : _____

With : _____

Difficulty : _____

Weather :

Notes/Thoughts/Memories

_____

_____

_____

_____

_____

_____

_____

_____

_____

I Give This Experience : ☆ ☆ ☆ ☆ ☆

Goal : _____

_____

🎒 What I need :

- ☐ _____
- ☐ _____
- ☐ _____
- ☐ _____
- ☐ _____
- ☐ _____
- ☐ _____

📋 Details :

Date : _____

Location : _____

Start Time : _____

End time : _____

With : _____

Difficulty : _____

Weather : ☀️ ⛅ 🌧️ 🌨️

Notes/Thoughts/Memories

_____

_____

_____

_____

_____

_____

_____

_____

I Give This Experience : ☆ ☆ ☆ ☆ ☆

Goal : _____

_____

What I need :

- [ ] _____
- [ ] _____
- [ ] _____
- [ ] _____
- [ ] _____
- [ ] _____
- [ ] _____

Details :

Date : _____

Location : _____

Start Time : _____

End time : _____

With : _____

Difficulty : _____

Weather :

Notes/Thoughts/Memories

_____
_____
_____
_____
_____
_____
_____
_____

I Give This Experience :

Goal : _____

What I need :

- ☐ _____
- ☐ _____
- ☐ _____
- ☐ _____
- ☐ _____
- ☐ _____
- ☐ _____

Details :

Date : _____

Location : _____

Start Time : _____

End time : _____

With : _____

Difficulty : _____

Weather :

Notes/Thoughts/Memories

_____

_____

_____

_____

_____

_____

_____

_____

I Give This Experience : ☆ ☆ ☆ ☆ ☆

Goal : _____

_____

What I need :

- [ ] _____
- [ ] _____
- [ ] _____
- [ ] _____
- [ ] _____
- [ ] _____
- [ ] _____

Details :

Date : _____

Location : _____

Start Time : _____

End time : _____

With : _____

Difficulty : _____

Weather : ☀ ⛅ 🌧 🌨

Notes/Thoughts/Memories

_____
_____
_____
_____
_____
_____
_____
_____
_____

I Give This Experience : ☆ ☆ ☆ ☆ ☆

Goal : _____

_____

What I need :

- [ ] _____
- [ ] _____
- [ ] _____
- [ ] _____
- [ ] _____
- [ ] _____
- [ ] _____

Details :

Date : _____

Location : _____

Start Time : _____

End time : _____

With : _____

Difficulty : _____

Weather : ☀ ⛅ 🌧 🌨

Notes/Thoughts/Memories

_____

_____

_____

_____

_____

_____

_____

_____

I Give This Experience : ☆ ☆ ☆ ☆ ☆

Goal : _____
_____

What I need :

- [ ] _____
- [ ] _____
- [ ] _____
- [ ] _____
- [ ] _____
- [ ] _____
- [ ] _____

Details :

Date : _____
Location : _____
Start Time : _____
End time : _____
With : _____
Difficulty : _____
Weather :

Notes/Thoughts/Memories

_____
_____
_____
_____
_____
_____
_____
_____

I Give This Experience : ☆ ☆ ☆ ☆ ☆

Goal : _____

_____

What I need :	**Details :**
☐ _____	Date : _____
☐ _____	Location : _____
☐ _____	Start Time : _____
☐ _____	End time : _____
☐ _____	With : _____
☐ _____	Difficulty : _____
☐ _____	Weather : ☀ ⛅ 🌧 🌨

Notes/Thoughts/Memories

_____

_____

_____

_____

_____

_____

_____

_____

I Give This Experience : ☆ ☆ ☆ ☆ ☆

Goal : _____

_____

What I need :

- ☐ _____
- ☐ _____
- ☐ _____
- ☐ _____
- ☐ _____
- ☐ _____
- ☐ _____

Details :

Date : _____

Location : _____

Start Time : _____

End time : _____

With : _____

Difficulty : _____

Weather : ☀ ⛅ 🌧 ❄

Notes/Thoughts/Memories

_____

_____

_____

_____

_____

_____

_____

_____

I Give This Experience : ☆ ☆ ☆ ☆ ☆

Goal : _____

What I need :

- ☐ _____
- ☐ _____
- ☐ _____
- ☐ _____
- ☐ _____
- ☐ _____
- ☐ _____

Details :

Date : _____
Location : _____
Start Time : _____
End time : _____
With : _____
Difficulty : _____
Weather : ☀ ⛅ 🌧 ❄

Notes/Thoughts/Memories

_____
_____
_____
_____
_____
_____
_____
_____

I Give This Experience : ☆ ☆ ☆ ☆ ☆

Goal : _____

_____

What I need :

- ☐ _____
- ☐ _____
- ☐ _____
- ☐ _____
- ☐ _____
- ☐ _____
- ☐ _____

Details :

Date : _____

Location : _____

Start Time : _____

End time : _____

With : _____

Difficulty : _____

Weather : ☀ ⛅ 🌧 ❄

Notes/Thoughts/Memories

_____

_____

_____

_____

_____

_____

_____

_____

_____

I Give This Experience : ☆ ☆ ☆ ☆ ☆

Goal : _____
_____

What I need :

- [ ] _____
- [ ] _____
- [ ] _____
- [ ] _____
- [ ] _____
- [ ] _____
- [ ] _____

Details :

Date : _____
Location : _____
Start Time : _____
End time : _____
With : _____
Difficulty : _____
Weather : ☀️ ⛅ 🌧️ ❄️

Notes/Thoughts/Memories

_____
_____
_____
_____
_____
_____
_____
_____

I Give This Experience : ☆ ☆ ☆ ☆ ☆

Goal : _____

_____

What I need :

- [ ] _____
- [ ] _____
- [ ] _____
- [ ] _____
- [ ] _____
- [ ] _____
- [ ] _____

Details :

Date : _____

Location : _____

Start Time : _____

End time : _____

With : _____

Difficulty : _____

Weather :

Notes/Thoughts/Memories

_____

_____

_____

_____

_____

_____

_____

_____

_____

I Give This Experience : ☆ ☆ ☆ ☆ ☆

Goal : _____

_____

What I need :	Details :
☐ _____	Date : _____
☐ _____	Location : _____
☐ _____	Start Time : _____
☐ _____	End time : _____
☐ _____	With : _____
☐ _____	Difficulty : _____
☐ _____	Weather : ☀ ⛅ 🌧 🌨

Notes/Thoughts/Memories

_____

_____

_____

_____

_____

_____

_____

_____

I Give This Experience : ☆ ☆ ☆ ☆ ☆

Goal : _____

_____

What I need :

- ☐ _____
- ☐ _____
- ☐ _____
- ☐ _____
- ☐ _____
- ☐ _____
- ☐ _____

Details :

Date : _____

Location : _____

Start Time : _____

End time : _____

With : _____

Difficulty : _____

Weather : ☀ ⛅ 🌧 ☁

Notes/Thoughts/Memories

_____

_____

_____

_____

_____

_____

_____

_____

I Give This Experience : ☆ ☆ ☆ ☆ ☆

Goal : _____

What I need :

- [ ] _____
- [ ] _____
- [ ] _____
- [ ] _____
- [ ] _____
- [ ] _____
- [ ] _____

Details :

Date : _____

Location : _____

Start Time : _____

End time : _____

With : _____

Difficulty : _____

Weather :

Notes/Thoughts/Memories

_____

_____

_____

_____

_____

_____

_____

_____

I Give This Experience : ☆ ☆ ☆ ☆ ☆

Goal : _____

_____

🎒 What I need :

- ☐ _____
- ☐ _____
- ☐ _____
- ☐ _____
- ☐ _____
- ☐ _____
- ☐ _____

📋 Details :

Date : _____

Location : _____

Start Time : _____

End time : _____

With : _____

Difficulty : _____

Weather : ☀️ ⛅ 🌧️ ❄️

Notes/Thoughts/Memories

_____

_____

_____

_____

_____

_____

_____

_____

I Give This Experience : ☆ ☆ ☆ ☆ ☆

Goal : _____

_____

What I need :

- ☐ _____
- ☐ _____
- ☐ _____
- ☐ _____
- ☐ _____
- ☐ _____
- ☐ _____

Details :

Date : _____

Location : _____

Start Time : _____

End time : _____

With : _____

Difficulty : _____

Weather : ☀ ⛅ 🌧 ❄

Notes/Thoughts/Memories

_____

_____

_____

_____

_____

_____

_____

_____

I Give This Experience : ☆ ☆ ☆ ☆ ☆

Goal : _____

_____

What I need :

- [ ] _____
- [ ] _____
- [ ] _____
- [ ] _____
- [ ] _____
- [ ] _____
- [ ] _____

Details :

Date : _____

Location : _____

Start Time : _____

End time : _____

With : _____

Difficulty : _____

Weather : ☀ ⛅ 🌧 ☁

Notes/Thoughts/Memories

_____

_____

_____

_____

_____

_____

_____

_____

_____

I Give This Experience : ☆ ☆ ☆ ☆ ☆

*Goal :*_____

_____

What I need :	*Details :*

☐ _____

☐ _____

☐ _____

☐ _____

☐ _____

☐ _____

☐ _____

Date : _____

Location : _____

Start Time : _____

End time : _____

With : _____

Difficulty : _____

Weather : ☀ ⛅ 🌧 🌨

Notes/Thoughts/Memories

_____

_____

_____

_____

_____

_____

_____

_____

I Give This Experience : ☆ ☆ ☆ ☆ ☆

Goal : _____

_____

What I need :

- ☐ _____
- ☐ _____
- ☐ _____
- ☐ _____
- ☐ _____
- ☐ _____
- ☐ _____

Details :

Date : _____

Location : _____

Start Time : _____

End time : _____

With : _____

Difficulty : _____

Weather : ☀ ☁ 🌧 ❄

Notes/Thoughts/Memories

_____

_____

_____

_____

_____

_____

_____

_____

I Give This Experience : ☆ ☆ ☆ ☆ ☆

Goal : _____

What I need :

- [ ] _____
- [ ] _____
- [ ] _____
- [ ] _____
- [ ] _____
- [ ] _____
- [ ] _____

Details :

Date : _____
Location : _____
Start Time : _____
End time : _____
With : _____
Difficulty : _____
Weather :

Notes/Thoughts/Memories

_____

_____

_____

_____

_____

_____

_____

_____

I Give This Experience : ☆ ☆ ☆ ☆ ☆

Goal : _____

_____

What I need :

- [ ] _____
- [ ] _____
- [ ] _____
- [ ] _____
- [ ] _____
- [ ] _____
- [ ] _____

Details :

Date : _____

Location : _____

Start Time : _____

End time : _____

With : _____

Difficulty : _____

Weather : ☀ ⛅ 🌧 🌨

Notes/Thoughts/Memories

_____
_____
_____
_____
_____
_____
_____
_____
_____

I Give This Experience : ☆ ☆ ☆ ☆ ☆

Goal : _____

_____

What I need :

- ☐ _____
- ☐ _____
- ☐ _____
- ☐ _____
- ☐ _____
- ☐ _____
- ☐ _____

Details :

Date : _____

Location : _____

Start Time : _____

End time : _____

With : _____

Difficulty : _____

Weather : ☀ ⛅ 🌧 🌨

Notes/Thoughts/Memories

_____

_____

_____

_____

_____

_____

_____

_____

_____

I Give This Experience : ☆ ☆ ☆ ☆ ☆

Goal : _____

_____

What I need :

- ☐ _____
- ☐ _____
- ☐ _____
- ☐ _____
- ☐ _____
- ☐ _____
- ☐ _____

Details :

Date : _____

Location : _____

Start Time : _____

End time : _____

With : _____

Difficulty : _____

Weather : ☀ ⛅ 🌧 ☁

Notes/Thoughts/Memories

_____

_____

_____

_____

_____

_____

_____

_____

_____

I Give This Experience : ☆ ☆ ☆ ☆ ☆

Goal : _____

_____

What I need :

- ☐ _____
- ☐ _____
- ☐ _____
- ☐ _____
- ☐ _____
- ☐ _____
- ☐ _____

Details :

Date : _____

Location : _____

Start Time : _____

End time : _____

With : _____

Difficulty : _____

Weather : ☀ ⛅ 🌧 ❄

Notes/Thoughts/Memories

_____

_____

_____

_____

_____

_____

_____

_____

I Give This Experience : ☆ ☆ ☆ ☆ ☆

Goal : _____

_____

🎒 **What I need :**	📋 **Details :**
☐ _____	Date : _____
☐ _____	Location : _____
☐ _____	Start Time : _____
☐ _____	End time : _____
☐ _____	With : _____
☐ _____	Difficulty : _____
☐ _____	Weather : ☀️ ⛅ 🌧️ ❄️

Notes/Thoughts/Memories

_____

_____

_____

_____

_____

_____

_____

_____

I Give This Experience : ☆ ☆ ☆ ☆ ☆

Goal : _____

_____

What I need :

- ☐ _____
- ☐ _____
- ☐ _____
- ☐ _____
- ☐ _____
- ☐ _____
- ☐ _____

Details :

Date : _____

Location : _____

Start Time : _____

End time : _____

With : _____

Difficulty : _____

Weather : ☀ ⛅ 🌧 ❄

Notes/Thoughts/Memories

_____

_____

_____

_____

_____

_____

_____

_____

I Give This Experience : ☆ ☆ ☆ ☆ ☆

Goal : _____

_____

What I need :

- [ ] _____
- [ ] _____
- [ ] _____
- [ ] _____
- [ ] _____
- [ ] _____
- [ ] _____

Details :

Date : _____

Location : _____

Start Time : _____

End time : _____

With : _____

Difficulty : _____

Weather : ☀ ⛅ 🌧 🌨

Notes/Thoughts/Memories

_____

_____

_____

_____

_____

_____

_____

_____

_____

_____

I Give This Experience : ☆ ☆ ☆ ☆ ☆

Goal :_____

_____

🎒 What I need :

- ☐ _____
- ☐ _____
- ☐ _____
- ☐ _____
- ☐ _____
- ☐ _____
- ☐ _____

📋 Details :

Date : _____

Location : _____

Start Time : _____

End time : _____

With : _____

Difficulty : _____

Weather : ☀️ ⛅ 🌧️ 🌨️

Notes/Thoughts/Memories

_____

_____

_____

_____

_____

_____

_____

_____

_____

I Give This Experience : ☆ ☆ ☆ ☆ ☆

Goal :_____

_____

What I need :

- ☐ _____
- ☐ _____
- ☐ _____
- ☐ _____
- ☐ _____
- ☐ _____
- ☐ _____

Details :

Date : _____
Location : _____
Start Time : _____
End time : _____
With : _____
Difficulty : _____
Weather : ☀ ⛅ 🌧 ❄

Notes/Thoughts/Memories

_____

_____

_____

_____

_____

_____

_____

_____

_____

I Give This Experience : ☆ ☆ ☆ ☆ ☆

Goal : _____

_____

What I need :

- [ ] _____
- [ ] _____
- [ ] _____
- [ ] _____
- [ ] _____
- [ ] _____
- [ ] _____

Details :

Date : _____

Location : _____

Start Time : _____

End time : _____

With : _____

Difficulty : _____

Weather : ☀ ⛅ ⛈ ☁❄

Notes/Thoughts/Memories

_____

_____

_____

_____

_____

_____

_____

_____

_____

I Give This Experience : ☆ ☆ ☆ ☆ ☆

Goal : _____

_____

What I need :

- ☐ _____
- ☐ _____
- ☐ _____
- ☐ _____
- ☐ _____
- ☐ _____
- ☐ _____

Details :

Date : _____

Location : _____

Start Time : _____

End time : _____

With : _____

Difficulty : _____

Weather : ☀ ⛅ 🌧 🌨

Notes/Thoughts/Memories

_____

_____

_____

_____

_____

_____

_____

_____

_____

I Give This Experience : ☆ ☆ ☆ ☆ ☆

Goal : _____

_____

What I need :

- [ ] _____
- [ ] _____
- [ ] _____
- [ ] _____
- [ ] _____
- [ ] _____
- [ ] _____

Details :

Date : _____

Location : _____

Start Time : _____

End time : _____

With : _____

Difficulty : _____

Weather :

Notes/Thoughts/Memories

_____

_____

_____

_____

_____

_____

_____

I Give This Experience : ☆ ☆ ☆ ☆ ☆

Goal :_____

_____

🎒 What I need :

- ☐ _____
- ☐ _____
- ☐ _____
- ☐ _____
- ☐ _____
- ☐ _____
- ☐ _____

📋 Details :

Date : _____

Location : _____

Start Time : _____

End time : _____

With : _____

Difficulty : _____

Weather : ☀️ ⛅ 🌧️ ❄️

Notes/Thoughts/Memories

_____

_____

_____

_____

_____

_____

_____

_____

_____

I Give This Experience : ☆ ☆ ☆ ☆ ☆

Goal : _____

What I need :

- [ ] _____
- [ ] _____
- [ ] _____
- [ ] _____
- [ ] _____
- [ ] _____
- [ ] _____

Details :

Date : _____
Location : _____
Start Time : _____
End time : _____
With : _____
Difficulty : _____
Weather : ☀ ☁ 🌧 ❄

Notes/Thoughts/Memories

_____
_____
_____
_____
_____
_____
_____
_____

I Give This Experience : ☆ ☆ ☆ ☆ ☆

Goal : _____

_____

What I need :

- [ ] _____
- [ ] _____
- [ ] _____
- [ ] _____
- [ ] _____
- [ ] _____
- [ ] _____

Details :

Date : _____

Location : _____

Start Time : _____

End time : _____

With : _____

Difficulty : _____

Weather : ☀ ⛅ 🌧 ❄

Notes/Thoughts/Memories

_____

_____

_____

_____

_____

_____

_____

_____

_____

_____

I Give This Experience : ☆ ☆ ☆ ☆ ☆

Goal : _____

_____

What I need :

- [ ] _____
- [ ] _____
- [ ] _____
- [ ] _____
- [ ] _____
- [ ] _____
- [ ] _____

Details :

Date : _____

Location : _____

Start Time : _____

End time : _____

With : _____

Difficulty : _____

Weather : ☀ ⛅ 🌧 ☁

Notes/Thoughts/Memories

_____

_____

_____

_____

_____

_____

_____

_____

I Give This Experience : ☆ ☆ ☆ ☆ ☆

Goal : _____

_____

What I need :

- ☐ _____
- ☐ _____
- ☐ _____
- ☐ _____
- ☐ _____
- ☐ _____
- ☐ _____

Details :

Date : _____

Location : _____

Start Time : _____

End time : _____

With : _____

Difficulty : _____

Weather : ☀ ⛅ ⛈ ❄

Notes/Thoughts/Memories

_____

_____

_____

_____

_____

_____

_____

_____

I Give This Experience : ☆ ☆ ☆ ☆ ☆

Goal : _____

What I need :

- ☐ _____
- ☐ _____
- ☐ _____
- ☐ _____
- ☐ _____
- ☐ _____
- ☐ _____

Details :

Date : _____

Location : _____

Start Time : _____

End time : _____

With : _____

Difficulty : _____

Weather : ☀ ⛅ 🌧 ❄

Notes/Thoughts/Memories

_____

_____

_____

_____

_____

_____

_____

I Give This Experience : ☆ ☆ ☆ ☆ ☆

Goal : _____
_____

What I need :

- ☐ _____
- ☐ _____
- ☐ _____
- ☐ _____
- ☐ _____
- ☐ _____
- ☐ _____

Details :

Date : _____
Location : _____
Start Time : _____
End time : _____
With : _____
Difficulty : _____
Weather : ☀ ⛅ 🌧 ❄

Notes/Thoughts/Memories

_____
_____
_____
_____
_____
_____
_____
_____
_____

I Give This Experience : ☆ ☆ ☆ ☆ ☆

Goal : _____

What I need :

- [ ] _____
- [ ] _____
- [ ] _____
- [ ] _____
- [ ] _____
- [ ] _____
- [ ] _____

Details :

Date : _____

Location : _____

Start Time : _____

End time : _____

With : _____

Difficulty : _____

Weather : ☀️ ⛅ 🌧️ 🌨️

Notes/Thoughts/Memories

_____

_____

_____

_____

_____

_____

_____

_____

_____

I Give This Experience : ☆ ☆ ☆ ☆ ☆

Goal : _____

_____

What I need :

- [ ] _____
- [ ] _____
- [ ] _____
- [ ] _____
- [ ] _____
- [ ] _____
- [ ] _____

Details :

Date : _____

Location : _____

Start Time : _____

End time : _____

With : _____

Difficulty : _____

Weather :

Notes/Thoughts/Memories

_____

_____

_____

_____

_____

_____

_____

_____

I Give This Experience : ☆ ☆ ☆ ☆ ☆

Goal :_____

What I need :

- ☐ _____
- ☐ _____
- ☐ _____
- ☐ _____
- ☐ _____
- ☐ _____
- ☐ _____

Details :

Date : _____
Location : _____
Start Time : _____
End time : _____
With : _____
Difficulty : _____
Weather : ☀ ⛅ 🌧 ❄

Notes/Thoughts/Memories

_____
_____
_____
_____
_____
_____
_____
_____

I Give This Experience : ☆ ☆ ☆ ☆ ☆

Goal : _____

_____

What I need :

- ☐ _____
- ☐ _____
- ☐ _____
- ☐ _____
- ☐ _____
- ☐ _____
- ☐ _____

Details :

Date : _____

Location : _____

Start Time : _____

End time : _____

With : _____

Difficulty : _____

Weather : ☀ ⛅ 🌧 ❄

Notes/Thoughts/Memories

_____

_____

_____

_____

_____

_____

_____

_____

_____

I Give This Experience : ☆ ☆ ☆ ☆ ☆

Goal : _____

What I need :

- [ ] _____
- [ ] _____
- [ ] _____
- [ ] _____
- [ ] _____
- [ ] _____
- [ ] _____

Details :

Date : _____

Location : _____

Start Time : _____

End time : _____

With : _____

Difficulty : _____

Weather :

Notes/Thoughts/Memories

_____

_____

_____

_____

_____

_____

_____

_____

I Give This Experience : ☆ ☆ ☆ ☆ ☆

Goal : _____

_____

What I need :

- [ ] _____
- [ ] _____
- [ ] _____
- [ ] _____
- [ ] _____
- [ ] _____
- [ ] _____

Details :

Date : _____

Location : _____

Start Time : _____

End time : _____

With : _____

Difficulty : _____

Weather :

Notes/Thoughts/Memories

_____
_____
_____
_____
_____
_____
_____
_____
_____
_____

I Give This Experience : ☆ ☆ ☆ ☆ ☆

Goal : _____

What I need :

- [ ] _____
- [ ] _____
- [ ] _____
- [ ] _____
- [ ] _____
- [ ] _____
- [ ] _____

Details :

Date : _____
Location : _____
Start Time : _____
End time : _____
With : _____
Difficulty : _____
Weather : ☀ ⛅ 🌧 ❄

Notes/Thoughts/Memories

_____
_____
_____
_____
_____
_____
_____
_____
_____

I Give This Experience : ☆ ☆ ☆ ☆ ☆

Goal : _____

_____

What I need :

- ☐ _____
- ☐ _____
- ☐ _____
- ☐ _____
- ☐ _____
- ☐ _____
- ☐ _____

Details :

Date : _____
Location : _____
Start Time : _____
End time : _____
With : _____
Difficulty : _____
Weather : ☀ ⛅ 🌧 ❄

Notes/Thoughts/Memories

_____
_____
_____
_____
_____
_____
_____
_____

I Give This Experience : ☆ ☆ ☆ ☆ ☆

Goal : _____

_____

What I need :

- [ ] _____
- [ ] _____
- [ ] _____
- [ ] _____
- [ ] _____
- [ ] _____
- [ ] _____

Details :

Date : _____
Location : _____
Start Time : _____
End time : _____
With : _____
Difficulty : _____
Weather :

Notes/Thoughts/Memories

_____

_____

_____

_____

_____

_____

_____

_____

I Give This Experience : ☆ ☆ ☆ ☆ ☆

Goal : _____

🎒 What I need :

- ☐ _____
- ☐ _____
- ☐ _____
- ☐ _____
- ☐ _____
- ☐ _____
- ☐ _____

📋 Details :

Date : _____

Location : _____

Start Time : _____

End time : _____

With : _____

Difficulty : _____

Weather : ☀️ ⛅ 🌧️ 🌨️

Notes/Thoughts/Memories

_____

_____

_____

_____

_____

_____

_____

_____

I Give This Experience : ☆ ☆ ☆ ☆ ☆

Goal : _____

_____

What I need :

- [ ] _____
- [ ] _____
- [ ] _____
- [ ] _____
- [ ] _____
- [ ] _____
- [ ] _____

Details :

Date : _____

Location : _____

Start Time : _____

End time : _____

With : _____

Difficulty : _____

Weather :

Notes/Thoughts/Memories

_____

_____

_____

_____

_____

_____

_____

_____

I Give This Experience : ☆ ☆ ☆ ☆ ☆

Goal : _____

🎒 What I need :

- [ ] _____
- [ ] _____
- [ ] _____
- [ ] _____
- [ ] _____
- [ ] _____
- [ ] _____

📋 Details :

Date : _____
Location : _____
Start Time : _____
End time : _____
With : _____
Difficulty : _____
Weather : ☀️ ⛅ 🌧️ ❄️

Notes/Thoughts/Memories

_____
_____
_____
_____
_____
_____
_____
_____
_____

I Give This Experience : ☆ ☆ ☆ ☆ ☆

Goal : _____

_____

What I need :	**Details :**
☐ _____	Date : _____
☐ _____	Location : _____
☐ _____	Start Time : _____
☐ _____	End time : _____
☐ _____	With : _____
☐ _____	Difficulty : _____
☐ _____	Weather : ☀ ⛅ 🌧 ❄

Notes/Thoughts/Memories

_____

_____

_____

_____

_____

_____

_____

_____

I Give This Experience : ☆ ☆ ☆ ☆ ☆

Goal : _____

What I need :

- ☐ _____
- ☐ _____
- ☐ _____
- ☐ _____
- ☐ _____
- ☐ _____
- ☐ _____

Details :

Date : _____

Location : _____

Start Time : _____

End time : _____

With : _____

Difficulty : _____

Weather : ☀ ⛅ 🌧 ☁

Notes/Thoughts/Memories

_____

_____

_____

_____

_____

_____

_____

_____

I Give This Experience : ☆ ☆ ☆ ☆ ☆

Goal : _____

_____

 🎒 **What I need :**	📋 **Details :**

☐ _____

☐ _____

☐ _____

☐ _____

☐ _____

☐ _____

☐ _____

Date : _____

Location : _____

Start Time : _____

End time : _____

With : _____

Difficulty : _____

Weather : ☀ ⛅ 🌧 ❄

Notes/Thoughts/Memories

_____

_____

_____

_____

_____

_____

_____

_____

_____

I Give This Experience : ☆ ☆ ☆ ☆ ☆

Goal : _____

_____

What I need :

- ☐ _____
- ☐ _____
- ☐ _____
- ☐ _____
- ☐ _____
- ☐ _____
- ☐ _____

Details :

Date : _____

Location : _____

Start Time : _____

End time : _____

With : _____

Difficulty : _____

Weather : ☀ ⛅ 🌧 ❄

Notes/Thoughts/Memories

_____

_____

_____

_____

_____

_____

_____

_____

I Give This Experience : ☆ ☆ ☆ ☆ ☆

Goal : _____

What I need :

- [ ] _____
- [ ] _____
- [ ] _____
- [ ] _____
- [ ] _____
- [ ] _____
- [ ] _____

Details :

Date : _____

Location : _____

Start Time : _____

End time : _____

With : _____

Difficulty : _____

Weather : ☀ ⛅ 🌧 ❄

Notes/Thoughts/Memories

_____

_____

_____

_____

_____

_____

_____

_____

I Give This Experience : ☆ ☆ ☆ ☆ ☆

Goal : _____

_____

What I need :

- [ ] _____
- [ ] _____
- [ ] _____
- [ ] _____
- [ ] _____
- [ ] _____
- [ ] _____

Details :

Date : _____
Location : _____
Start Time : _____
End time : _____
With : _____
Difficulty : _____
Weather : ☀ ⛅ 🌧 🌨

Notes/Thoughts/Memories

_____
_____
_____
_____
_____
_____
_____
_____
_____

I Give This Experience : ☆ ☆ ☆ ☆ ☆

Goal :_____

_____

What I need :

- [ ] _____
- [ ] _____
- [ ] _____
- [ ] _____
- [ ] _____
- [ ] _____
- [ ] _____

Details :

Date : _____

Location : _____

Start Time : _____

End time : _____

With : _____

Difficulty : _____

Weather :

Notes/Thoughts/Memories

_____

_____

_____

_____

_____

_____

_____

_____

I Give This Experience : ☆ ☆ ☆ ☆ ☆

Goal : _____

_____

What I need :

- [ ] _____
- [ ] _____
- [ ] _____
- [ ] _____
- [ ] _____
- [ ] _____
- [ ] _____

Details :

Date : _____

Location : _____

Start Time : _____

End time : _____

With : _____

Difficulty : _____

Weather : ☀ ⛅ 🌧 ❄

Notes/Thoughts/Memories

_____

_____

_____

_____

_____

_____

_____

_____

_____

I Give This Experience : ☆ ☆ ☆ ☆ ☆

Goal : _____

_____

What I need :

- [ ] _____
- [ ] _____
- [ ] _____
- [ ] _____
- [ ] _____
- [ ] _____
- [ ] _____

Details :

Date : _____

Location : _____

Start Time : _____

End time : _____

With : _____

Difficulty : _____

Weather :

Notes/Thoughts/Memories

_____

_____

_____

_____

_____

_____

_____

_____

I Give This Experience : ☆ ☆ ☆ ☆ ☆

Goal :_____

What I need :

- ☐ _____
- ☐ _____
- ☐ _____
- ☐ _____
- ☐ _____
- ☐ _____
- ☐ _____

Details :

Date : _____
Location : _____
Start Time : _____
End time : _____
With : _____
Difficulty : _____
Weather : ☀ ⛅ 🌧 🌨

Notes/Thoughts/Memories

_____
_____
_____
_____
_____
_____
_____
_____

I Give This Experience : ☆ ☆ ☆ ☆ ☆

Goal : _____

_____

What I need :	Details :
☐ _____	Date : _____
☐ _____	Location : _____
☐ _____	Start Time : _____
☐ _____	End time : _____
☐ _____	With : _____
☐ _____	Difficulty : _____
☐ _____	Weather : ☀ ⛅ 🌧 ❄

Notes/Thoughts/Memories

_____

_____

_____

_____

_____

_____

_____

_____

I Give This Experience : ☆ ☆ ☆ ☆ ☆

Goal :_____

_____

What I need :

- [ ] _____
- [ ] _____
- [ ] _____
- [ ] _____
- [ ] _____
- [ ] _____
- [ ] _____

Details :

Date : _____

Location : _____

Start Time : _____

End time : _____

With : _____

Difficulty : _____

Weather :

Notes/Thoughts/Memories

_____

_____

_____

_____

_____

_____

_____

_____

_____

_____

I Give This Experience : ☆ ☆ ☆ ☆ ☆

Goal : _____

_____

What I need :

- ☐ _____
- ☐ _____
- ☐ _____
- ☐ _____
- ☐ _____
- ☐ _____
- ☐ _____

Details :

Date : _____

Location : _____

Start Time : _____

End time : _____

With : _____

Difficulty : _____

Weather : ☀ ⛅ 🌧 ❄

Notes/Thoughts/Memories

_____

_____

_____

_____

_____

_____

_____

_____

I Give This Experience : ☆ ☆ ☆ ☆ ☆

Goal : _____

_____

What I need :

- ☐ _____
- ☐ _____
- ☐ _____
- ☐ _____
- ☐ _____
- ☐ _____
- ☐ _____

Details :

Date : _____

Location : _____

Start Time : _____

End time : _____

With : _____

Difficulty : _____

Weather :

Notes/Thoughts/Memories

_____

_____

_____

_____

_____

_____

_____

_____

_____

I Give This Experience : ☆ ☆ ☆ ☆ ☆

Goal : _____

_____

What I need :

- ☐ _____
- ☐ _____
- ☐ _____
- ☐ _____
- ☐ _____
- ☐ _____
- ☐ _____

Details :

Date : _____

Location : _____

Start Time : _____

End time : _____

With : _____

Difficulty : _____

Weather :

Notes/Thoughts/Memories

_____

_____

_____

_____

_____

_____

_____

_____

I Give This Experience : ☆ ☆ ☆ ☆ ☆

Goal :_____

_____

🎒 What I need :

- ☐ _____
- ☐ _____
- ☐ _____
- ☐ _____
- ☐ _____
- ☐ _____
- ☐ _____

📋 Details :

Date : _____

Location : _____

Start Time : _____

End time : _____

With : _____

Difficulty : _____

Weather : ☀️ ⛅ 🌧️ ☁️

Notes/Thoughts/Memories

_____

_____

_____

_____

_____

_____

_____

_____

_____

I Give This Experience : ☆ ☆ ☆ ☆ ☆

Goal : _____

What I need :

- ☐ _____
- ☐ _____
- ☐ _____
- ☐ _____
- ☐ _____
- ☐ _____
- ☐ _____

Details :

Date : _____
Location : _____
Start Time : _____
End time : _____
With : _____
Difficulty : _____
Weather : ☀ ⛅ ⛈ ❄

Notes/Thoughts/Memories

_____
_____
_____
_____
_____
_____
_____
_____

I Give This Experience : ☆ ☆ ☆ ☆ ☆

Goal : _____

_____

What I need :

- [ ] _____
- [ ] _____
- [ ] _____
- [ ] _____
- [ ] _____
- [ ] _____
- [ ] _____

Details :

Date : _____

Location : _____

Start Time : _____

End time : _____

With : _____

Difficulty : _____

Weather : ☀ ⛅ 🌧 ❄

Notes/Thoughts/Memories

_____

_____

_____

_____

_____

_____

_____

_____

_____

I Give This Experience : ☆ ☆ ☆ ☆ ☆

Goal : _____

_____

🎒 What I need :

- ☐ _____
- ☐ _____
- ☐ _____
- ☐ _____
- ☐ _____
- ☐ _____
- ☐ _____

📋 Details :

Date : _____

Location : _____

Start Time : _____

End time : _____

With : _____

Difficulty : _____

Weather : ☀ ⛅ 🌧 ❄

Notes/Thoughts/Memories

_____

_____

_____

_____

_____

_____

_____

_____

_____

I Give This Experience : ☆ ☆ ☆ ☆ ☆

Goal : _____

_____

What I need :

- ☐ _____
- ☐ _____
- ☐ _____
- ☐ _____
- ☐ _____
- ☐ _____
- ☐ _____

Details :

Date : _____

Location : _____

Start Time : _____

End time : _____

With : _____

Difficulty : _____

Weather : ☀ ⛅ 🌧 ❄

Notes/Thoughts/Memories

_____

_____

_____

_____

_____

_____

_____

_____

I Give This Experience : ☆ ☆ ☆ ☆ ☆

Goal : _____

_____

🎒 What I need :

- [ ] _____
- [ ] _____
- [ ] _____
- [ ] _____
- [ ] _____
- [ ] _____
- [ ] _____

📋 Details :

Date : _____

Location : _____

Start Time : _____

End time : _____

With : _____

Difficulty : _____

Weather : ☀️ ⛅ 🌧️ ❄️

Notes/Thoughts/Memories

_____

_____

_____

_____

_____

_____

_____

_____

I Give This Experience : ☆ ☆ ☆ ☆ ☆

Goal : _____

_____

What I need :

- [ ] _____
- [ ] _____
- [ ] _____
- [ ] _____
- [ ] _____
- [ ] _____
- [ ] _____

Details :

Date : _____

Location : _____

Start Time : _____

End time : _____

With : _____

Difficulty : _____

Weather : ☀ ⛅ 🌧 ❄

Notes/Thoughts/Memories

_____

_____

_____

_____

_____

_____

_____

_____

I Give This Experience : ☆ ☆ ☆ ☆ ☆

Goal : _____

_____

What I need :	Details :
☐ _____	Date : _____
☐ _____	Location : _____
☐ _____	Start Time : _____
☐ _____	End time : _____
☐ _____	With : _____
☐ _____	Difficulty : _____
☐ _____	Weather : ☀ ☁ 🌧 ❄

Notes/Thoughts/Memories

_____

_____

_____

_____

_____

_____

_____

_____

I Give This Experience : ☆ ☆ ☆ ☆ ☆

Goal : _____

_____

What I need :

- ☐ _____
- ☐ _____
- ☐ _____
- ☐ _____
- ☐ _____
- ☐ _____
- ☐ _____

Details :

Date : _____

Location : _____

Start Time : _____

End time : _____

With : _____

Difficulty : _____

Weather : ☀ ⛅ 🌧 ❄

Notes/Thoughts/Memories

_____

_____

_____

_____

_____

_____

_____

_____

_____

_____

I Give This Experience : ☆ ☆ ☆ ☆ ☆

Goal : _____

_____

What I need :

- [ ] _____
- [ ] _____
- [ ] _____
- [ ] _____
- [ ] _____
- [ ] _____
- [ ] _____

Details :

Date : _____

Location : _____

Start Time : _____

End time : _____

With : _____

Difficulty : _____

Weather : ☀ ⛅ 🌧 ❄

Notes/Thoughts/Memories

_____

_____

_____

_____

_____

_____

_____

_____

I Give This Experience : ☆ ☆ ☆ ☆ ☆

Goal : _____

_____

What I need :

- ☐ _____
- ☐ _____
- ☐ _____
- ☐ _____
- ☐ _____
- ☐ _____
- ☐ _____

Details :

Date : _____

Location : _____

Start Time : _____

End time : _____

With : _____

Difficulty : _____

Weather : ☀ ⛅ 🌧 ☁

Notes/Thoughts/Memories

_____

_____

_____

_____

_____

_____

_____

_____

_____

_____

_____

I Give This Experience : ☆ ☆ ☆ ☆ ☆

Goal : _____

_____

What I need :

- ☐ _____
- ☐ _____
- ☐ _____
- ☐ _____
- ☐ _____
- ☐ _____
- ☐ _____

Details :

Date : _____

Location : _____

Start Time : _____

End time : _____

With : _____

Difficulty : _____

Weather : ☀ ⛅ 🌧 ❄

Notes/Thoughts/Memories

_____

_____

_____

_____

_____

_____

_____

_____

I Give This Experience : ☆ ☆ ☆ ☆ ☆

Goal : _____

_____

🎒 What I need :

- ☐ _____
- ☐ _____
- ☐ _____
- ☐ _____
- ☐ _____
- ☐ _____
- ☐ _____

📋 Details :

Date : _____

Location : _____

Start Time : _____

End time : _____

With : _____

Difficulty : _____

Weather : ☀️ ⛅ 🌧️ 🌨️

Notes/Thoughts/Memories

_____

_____

_____

_____

_____

_____

_____

_____

I Give This Experience : ☆ ☆ ☆ ☆ ☆

Goal : _____

_____

What I need :

- ☐ _____
- ☐ _____
- ☐ _____
- ☐ _____
- ☐ _____
- ☐ _____
- ☐ _____

Details :

Date : _____
Location : _____
Start Time : _____
End time : _____
With : _____
Difficulty : _____
Weather : ☀ ⛅ 🌧 ❄

Notes/Thoughts/Memories

_____

_____

_____

_____

_____

_____

_____

_____

I Give This Experience : ☆ ☆ ☆ ☆ ☆

Goal : _____
_____

🎒 What I need :

- [ ] _____
- [ ] _____
- [ ] _____
- [ ] _____
- [ ] _____
- [ ] _____
- [ ] _____

📋 Details :

Date : _____
Location : _____
Start Time : _____
End time : _____
With : _____
Difficulty : _____
Weather : ☀️ ⛅ 🌧️ 🌨️

Notes/Thoughts/Memories

_____
_____
_____
_____
_____
_____
_____
_____
_____
_____

I Give This Experience : ☆ ☆ ☆ ☆ ☆

Goal : _____

What I need :

- [ ] _____
- [ ] _____
- [ ] _____
- [ ] _____
- [ ] _____
- [ ] _____
- [ ] _____

Details :

Date : _____
Location : _____
Start Time : _____
End time : _____
With : _____
Difficulty : _____
Weather :

Notes/Thoughts/Memories

_____
_____
_____
_____
_____
_____
_____
_____

I Give This Experience : ☆ ☆ ☆ ☆ ☆

Goal : _____
_____

What I need :

- ☐ _____
- ☐ _____
- ☐ _____
- ☐ _____
- ☐ _____
- ☐ _____
- ☐ _____

Details :

Date : _____
Location : _____
Start Time : _____
End time : _____
With : _____
Difficulty : _____
Weather : ☀ ⛅ 🌧 ❄

Notes/Thoughts/Memories

_____
_____
_____
_____
_____
_____
_____
_____
_____
_____

I Give This Experience : ☆ ☆ ☆ ☆ ☆

Goal : _____

_____

🎒 What I need :

- ☐ _____
- ☐ _____
- ☐ _____
- ☐ _____
- ☐ _____
- ☐ _____
- ☐ _____

📋 Details :

Date : _____

Location : _____

Start Time : _____

End time : _____

With : _____

Difficulty : _____

Weather : ☀️ ⛅ 🌧️ ❄️

Notes/Thoughts/Memories

_____

_____

_____

_____

_____

_____

_____

_____

I Give This Experience : ☆ ☆ ☆ ☆ ☆

Goal : _____

_____

What I need :

- ☐ _____
- ☐ _____
- ☐ _____
- ☐ _____
- ☐ _____
- ☐ _____
- ☐ _____

Details :

Date : _____

Location : _____

Start Time : _____

End time : _____

With : _____

Difficulty : _____

Weather : ☀ ⛅ 🌧 ❄

Notes/Thoughts/Memories

_____

_____

_____

_____

_____

_____

_____

_____

I Give This Experience : ☆ ☆ ☆ ☆ ☆

Goal : _____

🎒 What I need :

- ☐ _____
- ☐ _____
- ☐ _____
- ☐ _____
- ☐ _____
- ☐ _____
- ☐ _____

📋 Details :

Date : _____

Location : _____

Start Time : _____

End time : _____

With : _____

Difficulty : _____

Weather : ☀️ ⛅ 🌧️ ❄️

Notes/Thoughts/Memories

_____

_____

_____

_____

_____

_____

_____

_____

I Give This Experience : ☆ ☆ ☆ ☆ ☆

Goal : _____

_____

What I need :

- ☐ _____
- ☐ _____
- ☐ _____
- ☐ _____
- ☐ _____
- ☐ _____
- ☐ _____

Details :

Date : _____

Location : _____

Start Time : _____

End time : _____

With : _____

Difficulty : _____

Weather : ☀ ⛅ 🌧 ❄

Notes/Thoughts/Memories

_____

_____

_____

_____

_____

_____

_____

_____

_____

I Give This Experience : ☆ ☆ ☆ ☆ ☆

Printed in Great Britain
by Amazon